# Limerick Nation

*'Write a limerick!' urged IRON Press,*
*'And in it employ your address;*
*Taking care, if you can,*
*To make every line scan,*
*So you're bound to be met with success.'*

Andy Logan

# Limerick Nation
## The UK in Verse
### Editors: Eileen Jones, Peter Mortimer

First published 2014 by IRON Press
5 Marden Terrace
Cullercoats
North Shields
NE30 4PD
tel/fax +44(0)191 2531901
ironpress@blueyonder.co.uk
www.ironpress.co.uk

Cover image and design Brian Grogan
Page design Brian Grogan, Kate Jones

ISBN 978-0-9575032-3-6
Printed by Field Print Ltd
Boldon on Tyne

Typeset in Georgia 10 pt

IRON Press Books are distributed by Central Books
and represented by Inpress Books Ltd
Churchill House, 12 Mosley Street
Newcastle upon Tyne, NE1 1DE
Tel: 44(0) 191 2308104
www.inpressbooks.co.uk

Supported using public funding by

ARTS COUNCIL
ENGLAND

LOTTERY FUNDED

# Contents

# Foreword

MANY OF THE POETS SENDING SUBMISSIONS TO THIS BOOK EXPRESSED A LONG TERM, EVEN LIFE long affection for the limerick in their 'biogs' and accompanying letters. There's obviously still something satisfying about producing a poem in a recognisable form. And the limerick has a long history in English literature and in the press, as Irish drinking song choruses, as nonsense verse, as a popular bawdy form, and as political satire. As Glyn Rees points out in his impressively erudite introduction to *The Mammoth Book Of Limericks* (Robinson 2008) the limerick is possibly the only metric form that has its origins in the English language; it was employed by Shakespeare within some of his plays, and there are limericks by Swinburne, Tennyson and Kipling. And the limerick survives – in comprehensive anthologies collected by Rees and others, and in more specialist forms, such as Martin Roth's illustrated satirical limericks on the history of world literature, published in *The Independent on Sunday* and collected in *The Limerickiad* (Smokestack Books).

But it seemed to us that in spite of the above, of all the poetic forms the limerick now has the lowest reputation. Not sure we can remember seeing a limerick published in *Poetry Review* and you wouldn't put your money on any 'serious' poet including a limerick in a live reading; the poetry establishment can be sniffy about the form.

Perhaps much of this is the fault of limericks themselves. The form is essentially disrespectful, even taboo-breaking, but difficulty arises when the content veers towards reliance on childish smut, wallowing in the supposed titillation from rude names for body parts, bodily functions, or outlandish sexual behaviour at the expense of paying attention to the wit and the craft of the limerick form.

Chosen place names in limericks of this kind are usually arbitrary, more to do with a convenient rhyme than any geographical interest. While no one would want to make the limerick respectful, we were determined that in this place name anthology the form should be treated with the respect it deserves. Many of the limericks here use the context of their place to excellent effect. It was a stipulation to only consider limericks from the poet's place of residence (which is why we accepted only postal submissions, only with an SAE).

We found a lot of ingenuity. As well as the town or the city, some used the district, the county, the name of the street and even the post-code as the rhyme. If it formed part of their address (and was good) we allowed it and applauded the initiative.

There is a satisfying sense in these pages of the individuality of our Limerick UK. The attraction of the place name theme is indisputable; and editing the book has been a highly entertaining education in national geography and in some obscure facts about places and their names. Poets have risen to the challenges of finding a rhyme for Kirby Muxloe or Bosherston, and of exploiting to the full local city names such as Brizzle and Cambry and the quirky pronunciation of Frome or Huyton. We also gave the writers the chance to take a non-tourist-board approach in their thirty word maximum place description. Again, many took up the challenge to quirky effect.

What's clear throughout the anthology is the strength of the feelings people have towards the place where they live – some of the more positive descriptions might trigger a cynical response, but while we don't believe that's justified, depth of feeling is sometimes even more obvious in the downbeat and satirical descriptions – there's a hefty amount of rage expressed within these covers about the damage done to Shakespeare's birthplace, for example.

We have contributions from established writers and from new writers and it's good that some of the included poems are from people who are first time submitters of poetry: or those who write in other forms or genres, or usually write only for friends and family, but who have felt able to have a go at – or even subvert – something that despite its brevity and scope for humour can be an exacting form. To be fair to the form it is bad limericks that have established the unenviable side of its reputation. If this collection can contribute to promoting the positive side, by introducing a new generation of place name limericks that are witty, wise and imaginative, we shall be pleased. Putting together the anthology has been hard work, but a lot of fun. And poetry doesn't have enough fun. It seems there's something enduringly productive in linking the approachable and resilient if occasionally derided limerick with a subject that's one of the most inspiring for many writers – home.


**Eileen Jones, Peter Mortimer**
*Wylam and Cullercoats, Summer 2014*

# North East

Berwick-upon-Tweed
Blaydon
Cleadon
Corbridge
Cullercoats
Darras Hall
Dinnington
Dinnington Green
Forest Hall
Fulwell, Sunderland
Greenside
Harrogate
Hexham
Newburn
Newcastle upon Tyne
North Shields
Northumberland
Peterlee
Ryton
Stockton-on-Tees
Tyne and Wear
Wardley, Gateshead
Whitley Bay
York

# Madeline Bennett

## Corbridge, Northumberland

A fisherman hailing from Corbridge
Kept a box of fresh bait in his small fridge,
But the grubs crawled away
Into his paté,
Thus putting him right off his sandwich.

An ambitious young builder from Corbridge
Constructed a house with a drawbridge.
This feature of mention
Drew female attention
And thus it became his amour-bridge.

An eccentric dog-lover from Corbridge
Once took out a huge second mortgage
In order to purchase
Gold statues of lurchers
And canine-themed art even more kitsch.

A pasty-white man from Northumberland
To get his skin bronzed by the sun had planned,
So he lay out all week
Baking face, chest and feet,
While on weekends 'twas mostly his bum he tanned.

Nestled in the beautiful Tyne Valley near Hadrian's
Wall, the ancient Roman town of Corbridge is a small
but vibrant community with galleries, pubs, historic
buildings and wandering ducks.

# Nick Brigham

## Allendale Road, Hexham

The strange folk of Allendale Road,
are naked, except for blue woad;
they don't wear a stitch
and the paint makes them itch,
but the fashion is *so* à la mode.


The worshipful Mayor of Hexham
said, 'Why don't we twin up with Wrexham?
Names are almost the same.'
But the Welsh weren't so game
(knew that twinning with English would vex 'em).


Allendale Road is no more, no less, than a
breathless climb from the centre of Hexham
into the heart of Tynedale and the beauty of
the Northumberland countryside.

# Sylvia Bunting

## York

A guinea-fowl gourmet from York
Was offered a fully stuffed stork
But said, 'Taxidermy
Is failing to stir me;
I think I will settle for pork.'


A tentative twitcher from York
Set off to encounter the auk.
His hopes were in vain,
On the awkward terrain
The auk that he stalked was a stork.

Romans colonised, Vikings invaded, Saxons were
converted; Henry VIII terrorised, Charles I governed,
Richard III was *not* buried; Archbishops ruled,
merchants adventured, railways were engineered.
'York's history is England's history.'

# Anne Carmichael

## Northumberland

There was a young man from Northumberland,
Had a penchant for wearing a cummerbund.
In his dress suit and sash
He would cut a real dash
From the east coast over to Cumberland.

Northumberland: Wild and desolate in places. Towns
bustling with cars and shoppers. History. Castles. Quiet
beaches washed by a cold sea. Rolling hills. Sheep.
Heather. Lowlands. Cattle, crops and coal.

# Alastair Chadwin

## Newcastle upon Tyne

I hail from the town of Newcastle,
So pronounce it to rhyme with a tassel.
But some say Newcastle
And rhyme it with parcel.
The whole thing's a bit of a hassle.

Stretching happily on the north bank of the Tyne,
Newcastle remains riotously amused. Northernmost
city of England, once garrison town against Scotland,
happily suspicious of both.

# Steve Chettle

## Newburn

Whilst rowing the Tyne at Newburn
A chap hoped that his girlfriend could learn
That rowlocks and oar
Are not bad words (off-shore)
And therefore should cause no concern.

Newburn: hard on the river Tyne, with panoramic
views of the river valley (and rowing). Three rowing
clubs, connections to George Stephenson, railways and
the start of the English Civil War.

# Kitty Fitzgerald

## Cullercoats

A woman called Hannah from Cullercoats
spent most of her life on board fishing boats,
she caught fish, skinned and filleted,
top-tailed, fried and skilleted
then battered – uniquely – with curried oats.

Cullercoats is an ex-thriving fishing community,
once famous for salt and names like Zephania
Haddock. Winslow Homer painted the strong,
determined fisherwomen.

# Christine D. Goodwin

## Whitley Bay

The carousel horses of Whitley
Used to gallop around oh so pritley
When I asked them to stay
They answered me 'neigh'
The fairground's long gone, they said bittley.

'Bay' was added to the name 'Whitley' in 1902 to avoid confusion with Whitby. The distinctive Spanish City dome opened in 1910 and remains today, but the much loved funfair is no more.

# Oz Hardwick

## York

A musical butcher from York
Serenaded his bacon and pork.
To the gammon he'd sing so,
This piggy Domingo,
As he bashed out a tune with a fork.


A young motorcyclist from York
At each pelican crossing would balk.
At the flashing of amber
He would ride up the camber,
Dismount on the pavement and walk.

York is an ever-changing city. The Shambles is no
longer the street of butchers, though perhaps their
songs can still be heard, and the pedestrianisation can
be confusing. Please dismount.

# Doug Harris

## Stockton-on-Tees

A floosie of Stockton-on-Tees
Developed an awful disease,
Infecting as well
Her entire clientele.
We applaud her reduction in fees...

Once, a circus at Stockton-on-Tees
Performed in a terrible breeze.
The splash was a clue,
(Yes the river runs through).
The advert read, 'Vacant Trapeze'.

In the widest high street in the UK, Ridley Scott,
Thomas Sheraton and John Walker dreamed of their
movies, furniture and safety matches while folk arrived
on the world's first passenger railway...

# Hugh Hunter

## Cleadon

In this Seat of the Gods that is Cleadon,
We repose in a cultural Eden.
'Neath our Olympian Hill,
Oh we're so 'Lit & Phil'.
Upper Class? 'Darling do pass the Dijon.'

Cleadon Village: Well heeled if rather snooty part of
South Tyneside. Often the butt of witty remarks from
Shields folk. Does have a well-known hill, but
somewhat smaller than Olympus.

# Andy Logan

## Tyne & Wear

Yes it's true that I'm from Tyne & Wear
But there's one thing I find mighty queer:
That council's long gone,
There are councillors none.
Are we not just Northumbrians here?

Cullercoats, now in 'Tyne & Wear' was the village
where I spent my childhood years, a small, tightly
knit Northumbrian coastal community a stone's throw
from the resting place of Northumbrian kings.

# Margaret Nesbitt

## Berwick-upon-Tweed

If you go to Berwick-on-Tweed
You'll find the folks here are agreed
The road is too narrow
We don't drive a barrow
A dualled A1's what we need.

Beautiful Berwick is perched on the fence betwixt
England and Scotland protecting both countries from
invaders. It has yet to decide on which side of the fence
it really belongs!!

# Orian Norfolk

## Dinnington, Newcastle upon Tyne

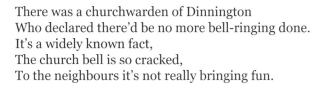

There was a churchwarden of Dinnington
Who declared there'd be no more bell-ringing done.
It's a widely known fact,
The church bell is so cracked,
To the neighbours it's not really bringing fun.


An Arctic explorer from Newcastle
Always said city life was a hassle.
But his mates in the bar
Fear he'll venture too far;
If bears don't devour him, a crevasse'll!


There was a brave lad, of the Tyne
and Wear county, who thought it so fine,
When out on the toon
The pavements were strewn
With young ladies who'd supped too much wine.


Dinnington – good neighbours, and a peaceful place to
return to from the city centre chaos. This is where my
children grew up, and where my garden delights me.

# Sean O'Brien

## Forest Hall

*Château-Forêt Pseudolimerick*

There is a place they call Château-Forêt,
Where absolutely nothing's happened yet.
Renounce the grim metropolis
For this deep green necropolis,
Or else piss off to Palmersville then, pet.

Forest Hall is a Newcastle suburb in North Tyneside,
bounded by Wallsend to the south, Longbenton to the
west, Killingworth to the north – and Palmersville.

# June Portlock

## Wardley, Gateshead

There once was a man from Wardley
Who found he could no longer see
So he had his eyes tested
But the price they requested
Made him shout, 'What a fraudulent fee!'


There was an old girl from Gateshead
Who wanted to dye her hair red
But the deep shade of rose
Matched her big nose
So she opted for purple instead.

Wardley was the site of a coal mine and retains the
friendliness of a pit village community. Living near to
Windy Nook in Gateshead is enough to bring the rose
to anyone's nose.

# Joanna Rimmer

## Tyne and Wear

A young maiden from Tyne and Wear
Had neighbours much tempted to leer.
It was not for her hips
Or the full scarlet lips
But the 'come hither' look of her rear.

Originally from the south, Joanna Rimmer now feels
more at home in Tyne than Wear. Although, as the
years go by, perhaps that should be more Wear than
Tear?

# Alison Ringrose

## Darras Hall

A young wife from hip Darras Hall
set out to stun husband and all.
She wore lots of bling
and indulged in a fling,
falling out of her dress at the Ball.

Green hedges, graceful trees, spacious gardens, dark
night skies, friendly people and the best baker's shop in
Northumberland – that's Darras Hall for me. I hope the
developers don't ruin it!

# Fiona Ritchie Walker

## Blaydon

A lovestruck young lady in Blaydon
proposed to her shy boyfriend, Aiden.
He ran off so quickly
and was last seen in Mickley,
but her passion for Aiden's not fadin'.


A runner from Blaydon-on-Tyne
went to Balmbra's to join the start line;
'twas the eighth day of June,
he'd arrived there too soon,
Blaydon's race date is nine – every time.


Blaydon, home to the famous races, is full of steep
streets, providing free cardio workouts, with bonus
views of the Tyne. Garibaldi lives in our library (well,
just his head).

# Chris Robinson

## Peterlee

Have you ever noticed how Peterlee
is made mostly of the letter 'e'?
Not one other vowel,
passes one's jowl,
when mouthing my home town, Peterlee

Peterlee was built as a new town for the (now former)
collieries of East Durham. It is home to Castle Eden
Dene and Victor Pasmore's Apollo Pavilion.

# Susan Routledge

## Hexham

There was a young man from Hexham
Whose work was with rabbits – he'd sex 'em
But he didn't know
A buck from a doe
Now there's bunnies from Hexham to Wrexham

The haunt of marauding Vikings 1300 years ago,
Hexham nowadays proudly holds the title of England's
favourite market town – as voted for by *Country Life*.

# Heather Russell

## Dinnington Green

A lady from Dinnington Green
When told that she looked like the Queen,
Enquired, with a frown,
'Then where is one's crown,
Not to mention one's smart limousine?'

With wide grass verges lined with flowering trees,
Dinnington Green is a well-kept secret – a quiet estate
tucked away near Newcastle Airport and on the road
between Gosforth and Ponteland.

# Josephine Scott

## Cullercoats

There once was a pirate from Cullercoats
Who decided to raid in a speedboat
It got stuck in top gear
And crashed into the pier
Now he runs soirées on his houseboat

Cliff House, the oldest building in Cullercoats, was used
to store smuggled goods. A secret passage, accessed by
a trapdoor in the study, leads down through the cliffs
and on to the beach.

# Helen Shay

## Harrogate

A famous crime writer ran away to Harrogate
To escape cad of a husband and marital fate.
She had treatments at the Turkish Baths
but sulphur water was no bundle of laughs.
So Agatha went home to divorce and celebrate.

Famous for Betty's Café and Fat Rascals, Harrogate is
not so 'genteel' a spa town. The sulphur water reeks of
bad eggs, and nightlife these days is raucous, even fun.

# David Stephenson

## Greenside, Ryton

A jaded couturier from Greenside,
whose wife was a bit on the lean side,
tried inflaming his passion
by bucking the fashion
and cutting the legs of her jeans wide.


A dedicated coffee drinker from Greenside,
who wanted to roast his own beans, cried:
'But I don't have the time
to grind them that fine!'
so he gave up and went back to freeze-dried.


A shy young fellow from Ryton
refused to make love with the light on.
But his girl didn't mind
'cos true love is blind
and a shot in the dark is excitin'.


The village of Greenside (postal town Ryton), is a
former mining community at the lower end of the Tyne
Valley. Although a semi-rural paradise, it's a tough
place for rhymers.

# Rob Walton

## North Shields, Tyne and Wear

There was a young actor from Shields
Who chased after Hollywood deals
He called in some favours
From dear Nigel Havers
And a bloke who once knew Ian Beale


There was an old woman from Tyne and Wear
Who found it most awfully difficult to adhere
To rules about scanning
That took too much planning
So she gave up the limerick-making malarkey and went
for a beer.

North Shields was originally a suburb of Paris, flown to
Tyneside for the North East Coast Exhibition of 1929.
It met and married a local man and decided to stay.

# Julian Wilkin

## Northumberland

There was a young lass from Northumberland,
Who went for a day trip to Sunderland.
She stepped off the train,
And fell down a drain,
And said, 'I'm like Alice in Wonderland!'

Northumberland – Reivers, rivers, Pennines, peat and
high moors. Cheviot, the coast, cobles, castles, kippers,
Kielder and coal. Empty golden beaches, sheep, song,
pipes and voices. The Wall, Lindisfarne – the people.

# Evelyn Ann Williams

## Fulwell

There once was a young lady from Fulwell
Who frequented a pub called the Blue Bell
When offered libation
It was no tribulation
But the outcome she knew only too well.

The Blue Bell pub has loyally served the community in
the Fulwell area of Sunderland since the 19th century.
It offers appetising food and drink and also a regular
book club and quiz night.

# Midlands

Coventry
Kirby Muxloe
Leicester
Morda
Nottingham
Oakham
Rutland
Stamford
Stratford-on-Avon
West Bridgford

# Julie Burke

## West Bridgford, Nottingham

A cricketer in West Bridgford
was so proud of the runs he had scored
that he streaked to the crease,
but they called the police
when his googly lit up the board.


A chap on a 'stag do' from Nottingham
by mistake caught the train back to Cottingham.
He awoke from his slumber
up north of the Humber...
and his clothes? He had simply forgotten 'em.

West Bridgford is probably most famous for Trent
Bridge Cricket Ground. Nottingham (originally
*Snottingham*) conceals around 500 man-made caves;
some are open to the public, including those attached
to Britain's oldest pub.

# Tracy Davidson

## Stratford-on-Avon

A young poet from Shakespeare's Stratford,
Became ever increasingly bored,
With tourists who said 'Brill'
About writings by Will
While her own work was largely ignored.

Stratford = Shakespeare's birthplace. Ugly theatre now
even uglier courtesy of a new useless tower. Once
thriving Town Square has been a disgrace for years.
Apart from that – lovely place to live!

# Helen Everett-Camplin

## Oakham, Rutland

There once was a woman in Oakham,
Whose networking 'friends' were just token.
They're on Facebook, it's true,
But she hadn't a clue
How to message or tag 'em or poke 'em.


There once was a butcher from Oakham,
Whose love for a girl stayed unspoken.
He once overheard her
Say 'All meat is murder!'
And thus was the butcher's heart broken.


A fisherman near Rutland Water
Had a rather promiscuous daughter.
She'd had numerous lovers,
Including three brothers,
But nobody's tackle had caught her.

Modest Rutland, smallest county in England, feels no
need to brag about its immense beauty. It simply draws
the discerning to it like a magnet, leaving the rest to
providence.

# Cindy George

## Coventry

There was a young student in Coventry
Who used a bizarre means of entry
Eschewing the door
He'd ooze up through the floor
So was banned from all boozers in Coventry.

Coventry used to be Convent-ry, where the nuns lived.
A lot of present-day residents prefer to think of it as
Coven-try, where the witches are from.

# Allison Heward

## Morda

A woebegone woman from Morda,
Of boots and of shoes was a hoarder.
Her cure for the blues –
Buying more Jimmy Choos,
Till her husband yelled, 'Stop, that's an order!'

Morda is a quiet Shropshire village with an industrial
history. Currently it is struggling to preserve its identity
by resisting the urban creep of its larger neighbour –
the market town of Oswestry.

# Rennie Parker

## Stamford

How unfortunate that I live in Stamford.
For rhyming there isn't a damnword.
At least it looks grand
Not like Heligoland
Or Chorlton-cum-Hardy or Wangford.


I live in a town south of Lincoln
With loads of old buildings to think on.
There's spires and towers
And meadows with flowers
But there aren't any seats you can drink on.

Stamford, Lincs. is an attractive stone town on the
River Welland, painted by Turner and praised by
Betjeman, among others. Not everyone who lives
here is posh.

# D. A. Prince

## Kirkby Muxloe, Leicester

Try suggesting a weekend in Leicester
and watch your *amour* turn protester.
It's all roadworks and cones,
and that dead king's old bones
aren't much of a romantic gesture.

Life's quiet within Kirby Muxloe
by the M1 where juggernaut trucks flow.
The castle's a ruin,
there isn't much doin'
'cept a moat where some wintering ducks go.

Before the discovery of Richard III's grave, Leicester
was more widely known as the home of Adrian Mole.
Kirby Muxloe Castle, begun by Lord Hastings, was left
unfinished after his execution by Richard III.

# Dennis Walker

## Oakham

Wrongdoers in the town of Oakham
Were put in the stocks till it broke 'em
But criminals more elite
Housed in Gaol street
Spent all their days picking oakum

Oakham stocks, situated under the market place
butter cross, are unique in having an odd number of leg
restraints, as the town's most persistent offender had a
wooden leg.

# East Anglia

Dersingham
Drayton

# Catherine Bailey

## Drayton

There was an inventor from Drayton,
Whose contraption was meant to can bacon;
But, one day he fell in,
And was sealed in a tin,
Now they're selling cheap bacon in Drayton!

Drayton is an historical suburban village in the county of Norfolk. With easy access to Norwich City, and the coastal regions, it is a super place to live.

# Lois Williams

## Dersingham

There was an old poet from Dersingham
Who tried to invent a new versingham:
Full rhymes or half
And all for a laugh,
But the critics' rebuff was too tersingham.

Dersingham is a pastureland village along Norfolk's
Wash coastline. Romans stopped here as did, perhaps,
the Domesday Book's scribe – Dersingham gets a
mention. Pretty carstone buildings, sunsets and
migrating geese.

# London

London E1
Chingford E4

# Annemarie Cooper

## London E1

An earnest young woman from E1
Was having far too much fun
She deemed earthly delights
Were for Saturday nights
For the rest it's cold showers for one

London E1 contains Cable Street, scene of the
resistance to the Blackshirts in the '30s; Radcliffe
Highway, popular with press gangs and foot pads
in the 18th Century; and Brick Lane.

# Gerda Mayer

## Chingford E4

Quoth the bard of Chingford E4
'Posterity, thee I implore:
On my semi-detached
Fix a firmly attached
Plaque with my name by the door.'

The cat who visits 12 Mar-
garet Ave's too ungrateful by far.
Though he laps double-cream
In a sort of a dream,
There's no 'thanks, you're a pal, you're a star!'

Said the old champ of Chingford E4,
'I'm not quite as blithe as before.
And Life's glamour and glitz
like my wits are in bits –
But my verses deserve an encore!'

Chingford is on the outskirts of London by Epping
Forest. Three streets of bungalows, with Hawks Wood
rising above. My semi-det. bungalow is squat and
slightly mildewed like its owner.

# South East

Canterbury
Chelmer Village
Chelmsford
Kent
Pinner
Rayners Lane
Rustington
Southend-on-Sea
Surrey
Tunbridge Wells

# Paula Balfe

## Southend-on-Sea

There once was a thoughtless Southender
Who spoke to his wife, warm and tender –
'Let me now feast my eyes
On your vast, lardy thighs!'
So she fashioned nut roast with a blender.


Said a postman from Southend-on-Sea,
'I know where I'd much rather be'
So he chucked all his mailings
Right over some railings
And hurried on home for his tea.

Southend-on-Sea – home of the world's longest pier,
and with the greatest global concentration of talented
litterbugs and rotund rears in lycra. But the natives are
friendly and their rottweilers very docile.

# Michael Charles

## Kent

The garden of England is Kent;
About that there is no argument.
Its fruit and its berries,
Its apples and cherries
Are what makes the nation content.

Kent has changed much since the days when Charles
Dickens walked through its orchards and fields, but it
can still lay claim to being the 'Garden of England'.

# Frances Chatt

## Flat 1, Surrey

*Herbalist*

A herbalist down in Flat 1
Grew her poisons in pots in the sun.
As a hobby she'd bake
Mixing hemlock in cake
Which she fed to her neighbours for fun.


*Commuter*

A City commuter from Surrey,
One morning got dressed in a hurry.
His sights were set high,
But his corporate tie
Was embossed with last night's chicken curry.


I retired to Croydon (?!!?) and most of my neighbours
commute. When I moved, my flat had a jungle outside
which I'm trying to tame into a herb garden.

# Simon John Cox

## Tunbridge Wells

A lance-corporal from Tunbridge Wells
Spent his army career dodging shells.
But the blasts were so close
He's now deaf as a post
And he listens to music by smell.

An editor from Tunbridge Wells
Broke his laptop, and P's became L's.
His boss, who saw red,
Sacked him right there and said:
'Clear your desk and inform Lersonnel.'

An explorer, Dardan, from T. Wells
Found a new route for his caravels.
He'd used Dardanays,
Dardanbees through to kays,
So he named it instead Dardanelles.

The wizards around Tunbridge Wells
Tend to cast rather middle-class spells.
They make tramps disappear,
Deli queues less severe,
And they turn all the cuisine nouvelle.

Officially Royal, home to Disgusted, and both as
conservative and Conservative as it comes, Tunbridge
Wells is the middle-Englander's middle England.

# Nicollette Foreman

## Chelmer Village

His address is within Chelmer Village
which technically *isn't* a village.
For make no mistake,
it's just an estate,
at the end of the day it's town spillage.

Even though Chelmsford City Football Club was formed
in 1938, the town was only awarded a city status for the
Queen's Diamond Jubilee in 2012.

# Dee Gordon

## Southend-on-Sea

Young Sarah from Southend-on-Sea,
Fed up giving favours for free,
Tried her luck in Thorpe Bay,
Where the posh people stay,
And charged an inordinate fee.

The longest pleasure pier in the world, yes,
but Southend is not, sadly, on Sea. It is
Southend-on-Thames. Or Southend-on-Mud.
But lovely with it.

# Anne Murphy

## Chelmsford

If ever you come to Chelmsford
(a city where culture's abhorred)
you'll find poets but three –
just her, her and me –
I think we deserve a reward!

Despite being over eight hundred years old,
Chelmsford still has no dedicated space for the arts,
not even a proper gallery – though it does have more
than one theatre.

# Marion Russell

## Kent

There was a young lady from Kent
Who never knew how much she spent
She went to Bluewater
Bought more than she oughta
And ended up owing the rent.

Kent has many faces: the garden of England, historic
cities, seaside towns, hop farms and oast houses
and big shopping centres like Bluewater built in
old quarries.

# Patricia Feinberg Stoner

## Rustington

Cried a flighty young lady of Rustington
'I've done all my chores, got my dusting done.
I'll go out on the pull.'
(Which she did, to the full,
Then returned with a smile, all her lusting done.)

Rustington-on-Sea is where Michael Flanders
encountered a gnu, and the mobility scooter is king.
Rustington was a South East in Bloom gold award
winner in 2013.

# John Whitworth

## Canterbury

When the folks throw a party in Cambry
They make it one hell of a jambry.
Yes, they get very merry
In old Canterbury
On cocktails of vodka and crambry.

The Cathedral of old Canterbury
Serves pints of sweet stout and dry sherry,
So when the Archbishop
Yells, 'Chrisht, what a pish up!'
He's not *slightly* drunk. No, he's very.

Canterbury, pronounced Cambry by its inhabitants,
Can-ter-bury by the ignorant, boasts a cathedral, two
railway stations and three universities. Wolves roam
the ancient Blean Forest, devouring unruly children.

# Kevin Wooldridge

## Rayners Lane, Pinner

A young lady from near Rayners Lane
Was bound for some sunshine in Spain.
The delayed flight from Heathrow
Was incredibly slow
So she spray-tanned herself on the plane.


A young city trader from Pinner
Saw himself as life's ultimate winner.
His achievements were legion
Known all over the region
But 'Mummy' still cooked him his dinner.

The original Pinner village in NW London dates from
1231. It hosts an annual street fair and has been home
to Mrs Beeton, Heath Robinson, Ronnie Barker, Elton
John and David 'Poirot' Suchet.

# South

Hampshire
New Forest
Southampton

# Sue Spiers

## Southampton

There was a young girl of Southampton
who climbed up a mountain in crampons
At high altitude
she sighed, 'Though it's crude
I'll soak up my nosebleed with tampons.'

Southampton, home of the merchant navy, sent the
Pilgrim Fathers off in the Mayflower and provided
eighty percent of the crew of RMS Titanic. Benny Hill
had a milk round here.

# Allison Symes

## Hampshire

One joy of living in Hampshire
Is knowing that not much is dire
The New Forest and Solent
And tourist traps of that bent
Keep the county out of the mire

The New Forest National Park has varied wildlife
thanks to its woodland, bogs, grassland and heathland.
The Solent coastline, including the New Forest, is a
Special Area of Conservation.

# Janet Turner

## New Forest, Hants

An old man in New Forest, Hants,
Went walking just wearing his pants.
The vicar came past him
And proceeded to blast him
With surprisingly blasphemous rants.

The New Forest is an area of ancient woodland,
commercial forestry and open moorland, where cattle
and ponies wander free, along with roe, fallow and red
deer. Absolute heaven!

# South West

Bristol
Burnham-on-Sea
Cornwall
Devon
Frome
Hereford
Somerset
Stoke Bishop
Swindon
Torquay

# Jerome Betts

## Torquay

The coastal resort of Torquay
Once delighted the *haute bourgeoisie*.
But is now looking shabby
Despite its old abbey
And bust of Dame Agatha C.

Riviera compared with Torquay?
Unlike Cannes in the slightest degree!
The Channel is cold
And the residents old
With an absence of Gallic *esprit*.

God's waiting-room, i.e. Torquay,
Provides views to accompany tea
Of villas and pines–
Yet the end of the line's
Not a prospect to fill you with glee.

Though the holiday trade of Torquay
Is far less than it once used to be
As all budgets grow leaner,
It can boast a marina
And an excellent Lib-Dem MP.

Torquay, 'The Queen of the English Riviera' or
Sinopolis of the South-West is Devon's largest seaside
resort. Though popular for retirement it is geologically
complex and far from flat.

# Maggie Bevan

## Devon

Tom Cobley of 6 Millford Road
Went out in the nude when it snowed.
He did it for swank
But his swanky bits shrank
And he sighed, 'Oi got froz – an' it showed.'

The natives of Widecombe, Devon
Bake only bread without leaven.
Their Widecombe fare
Is Doner Grey Mare –
This is true or my name isn't Bevan.

Don't you love EX10 8DR!
BS8 4JY's below par.
OX1 chills your blood.
HU2's dull as mud
And NE 3-0 is bizarre!

Nan Gurney of Crediton, Devon
Once more watches *Ocean's Eleven*
As she quaffs Blackthorn Dry
With her homity pie
She ascends with George Clooney to heaven.

Millford Road has houses one side and a small, polite
river the other, which occasionally roars down juggling
garden furniture and uprooted trees. That's when you
start carrying stuff upstairs.

# Phyllis Higgins

## Frome

There was a brash lady from Frome.
Loud voiced, she'd blare, bellow and boom.
But how Fate can spite us!
She caught laryngitis
And now she's as quiet as the tomb.


A dog that was long lost in Frome
Was craving some scraps to consume.
His life was quite hard
Till in a graveyard
He found his old chum to exhume.


A literary lady from Frome
Sighed, 'Life is just all doom and gloom.
I long to be published,
Not put on a slush list.
I just need a good *nom de plume.*'


Frome is no 'clone town', but has its own character.
It is a place where history and the modern world blend
together. All aspects of the arts thrive here.

# Moira Quinn

## Cornwall

A grisly old sea dog from Cornwall
was rounding the cliffs in a white squall.
It blew him off course
with such terrible force
that he ended up landlocked in Walsall.


A flat-footed Pirate from Cornwall
danced a hornpipe and jig at the town hall.
He also sang shanties
whilst drinking chianties,
to a chorus of booing and catcalls.

I live on the edge, in the wilds of West Cornwall.
Penzance is the end of the line: the place where
everybody stops when they can't go any further.

# Caroline Rose

## Frome

By moonlight a sorceress of Frome
Would ride round the skies on a broom.
But really this mover
Just longed for a Hoover
Because that has more vra vra vroom!

Historic Frome, home to anyone with lots to say, is
where a man can walk about with an enormous
python round his neck, and no-one finds it odd!

# Jill Sharp

## Swindon

Culture is thriving in Swindon
and, though we're not *Unter den Linden*,
it wasn't great luck
to be twinned with a Duck
When the Donald we wanted was Sinden.


The creative oasis of Swindon
is often derided and grinned on
by smart-alec folk
who think we're a joke
when it's them that the tail should be pinned on.

Minutes from the ancient Ridgeway path, Swindon,
twinned with Disney World, has a Literature Festival
every spring, its own dance studios, a world-class art
collection, a monthly poetry open mic, a thriving arts
centre...

# Janet Lesley Smith

## Frome, Somerset

An Italian man visiting Frome,
When informed the town's name rhymed with 'zoom',
Said, '*O mamma mia*,
These English are queer,
I expect they pronounce Rome as 'Room!'

A vivacious young barmaid in Frome
Told admirers, who bought her perfume,
'I find scent a turn-off,
But buy me iced Smirnoff,
And you'll turn on this girl's va-va-voom!'

At a funeral, the Vicar of Frome
Opened up the deceased's family tomb,
And despite lack of space,
Found a suitable place,
Though the corpse only had standing room.

Some stage actors who play folk from Somerset
Use the comedy accents of Mummerset.
Though the natives object,
Many people suspect
They belong to the West Country's dumber set.

Frome is a small market town in Somerset, once
famous for a thriving textile industry; now better
known for its mediaeval streets and many arts and
crafts shops.

# Natalie Smith

## Bristol

*Leftovers*

An unmarried cook from Brizzle
Liked to fill her spag bol up with gristle.
She met a lush man,
Who stared into her pan.
But he left. Pretty quick. She's a miss. Still.


*Point Blank*

There was a male stripper from Bristol
Who quaffed cider from lead crystal.
After a gig as James Bond
He trapped off with a blonde
But was too drunk to fire his pistol.

> Bristol was recently voted best British city in which to live. One factor was the people who live here. These limericks are dedicated to two of them. Perhaps they should meet?

# Helen Somers

## Burnham-on-Sea

I am thinking that Burnham-on-Sea
Is a limerick certainty
It would be a shame
To deny it such fame
So do it for Burnham and me.

Burnham-on-Sea has a seven mile beach, England's
shortest pier, a leaning church tower and a Winter
Carnival. Its High Street consists of cafés, charity shops
and hairdressers. And a fishmonger!

# Bob Turvey

## Stoke Bishop

A very young cook from Stoke Bishop
Had a fish dish he would freely dish up
But the taste of his tuna
Would, later or sooner,
Cause diners to bring all the fish up.

Stoke Bishop: sleepy leafy Bristol suburb; too many house extensions and garden in-fills; was part of most educated Parliamentary constituency; harbour once used to flense whales; hugely tidal river.

# Jane Wheble

## Hereford

There once was a lady from Hereford
Who thought the cathedral was very good,
But the old Mundi map
Was a little bit crap
When getting directions to Stanford.

Hereford, a classic city – beautiful cathedral, river
with ancient bridge, independent shops, interesting
architecture, plaza style centre. So why build the
gigantic ugly shopping mall next door?

# Wales

Bosherston
Rhos on Sea

# Mary Halliwell

## Rhos on Sea

A lady from Rhos on Sea
Got bitten in bed by a flea,
But she wasn't upset,
She made it her pet –
It eats biscuits and sits on her knee.


If you're visiting Rhos on Sea
Please pronounce its name accurately.
Don't make people cross
By calling it 'Ross'
Or they'll send you to LlanfairPG.

Rhos on Sea is reputedly the place where old
Lancastrians go to die; but they can also live a little,
enjoying interesting shops and restaurants and fine
coastal walks.

# Shirley Hammond-Williams

## Bosherston

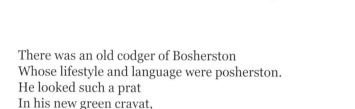

There was an old codger of Bosherston
Whose lifestyle and language were posherston.
He looked such a prat
In his new green cravat,
And was lynched when they heard him say, 'Gosherston!'

Bosherston is a small, unpretentious West Wales
village within the Pembrokeshire Coast National Park.
Famous for its beautiful lily ponds, it is dependent for its
survival on agriculture and tourism.

# North West

Boughton
Burton in Kendal
Cheshire
Chester
Hale
Huyton
Lancashire
Levenshulme
Liverpool
Lytham St Annes

# Jane Allsop

## Mowbray Drive, Burton in Kendal

A shirker from Mowbray Drive
Ate pies in his bed to survive
Watched daytime TV
Used a bottle to pee
And for muscle strength learnt how to jive.


A boffin from Burton in Kendal
Admired the findings of Mendel
He grew hybrid plants
In a pot of his Aunt's
And his vicious bees caused quite a skendel.

Burton in Kendal: a coaching village at the edge of the
Lakes. Once possessed of several hostelries frequented
by Wordsworth, prior to his arrest here for being drunk
and disorderly.

# Sue Barnard

## Hale

A wannabe poet from Hale
writes verse that's beyond the pale.
Her vocab's precocious,
her rhyming's atrocious,
so bard-wise, she's certain to fail.

Hale (situated between Altrincham and Wilmslow) is a
pleasant leafy suburb of South Manchester. It is known
to its residents as 'Hale Village' because of its strong
community atmosphere.

# David Bateman

## Gambier Terrace, Liverpool

On the Terrace, we're Liverpool 1,
And our poshness is second to none.
No we're *not* in L8:
That's beyond the back gate
(And the kink where the boundaries run).


From the splendour of Gambier Terrace
You can nearly see clear to Llanberis.
The view's only smirch
Is that bloody great church.
We'd shift it, if only they'd lerrus.

Gambier Terrace is up the hill from Liverpool centre.
It faces west towards the Wirral *if* you can see past
Liverpool Cathedral. There really *is* a kink in the
boundary of Liverpool 1 to accommodate the terrace.

# John Calvert

## Levenshulme

A Freudian from Levenshulme
Who seldom emerged from his room
Painted everything red
Then coiled up on the bed
And wished he was back in the womb


A pessimist from Levenshulme
Saw a world that was tainted in gloom
When told 'Have a nice day'
Said 'Please go away'
As he went off, predicting their doom

Levenshulme, where the long gullet of the A6 slowly
digests its intake of Irish stout, Asian spice, Polish
bread and Caribbean fruit whilst the world passes the
takeaways and coffee cafés on the 192 bus.

# David Crossley

## Lytham St Annes

There was a young man from Lytham,
Who made money from having no rhythm.
He enrolled in a choir,
But was flat as a tyre,
So they paid him not to sing with 'em.

Lytham is a town on the Lancashire Fylde Coast.
Champion of Britain in Bloom and described by the
Royal Horticultural Society as 'one of the greenest,
cleanest and most beautiful places in Britain'.

# Christine Henderson

## LA5 9XA, Lancashire

From zone LA5 9XA
A horse went exploring one day.
He wanted to see
If in zone 9XB
There'd be very much tastier hay.


A lassie from Lancashire County
Ran off for the day with a Mountie.
She told Mum and Dad,
'We haven't been bad.
He just had a taste of my Bounty.'

Between Morecambe Bay and the Lake District,
Carnforth is mainly noted for its railway station. Scenes
from *Brief Encounter* were filmed there, and it was
once a busy junction.

# Gordon Hill

## Huyton

There are no sandy beaches in Huyton
No elegant seafront like Brighton
Our main claim to fame's
Our peculiar name
It's not pronounced Hoyton it's Hyton.


A writer of horror from Huyton
Said 'My books are intended to frighten.
They may seem mediocre
Compared to Bram Stoker
But they sure as hell aren't Enid Blyton.'


I'm in L36 5UJ
So what? I can hear people say
Well, our postcodes define
For those insurance swine
What mammoth premiums we'll pay.


Huyton is a suburb of Liverpool, and until WW2 was
a small semi-agricultural community. In the forties it
was designated as an overspill area. The population
increased by 50,000.

# Jim Lewis

## Boughton, Chester, Cheshire

A fellow who once lived in Boughton
Didn't know undergarments had caught on
And he liked Dr Seuss
So his penis swung loose
Like the trunk of the Who-hearing Horton


A woman moved over from Chester
To a park in the city of Leicester
The complete lack of walls
Didn't thrill her at all
In fact it completely depressed her


There was a young artist from Cheshire
Who wished his ideas were much fresher
But being a jerk
Stuck to ripping off work
By Dali, Picasso and Escher


Chester is one of the few places you can enjoy
Victorian-built Tudor architecture from the comfort
of a Roman fort. Boughton sits just outside the walls,
overlooking the River Dee.

# Scotland

Edinburgh
Elderslie
Fife
Gourdon
Johnshaven
Kirriemuir
Montrose
Newport-on-Tay
Paisley

# Stephanie Arsoska

## Kirriemuir

There once was a young lass from Kirrie
who got herself into a tizzy.
She wanted straight hair,
chopped it all off with flair,
then cried, 'I was better off frizzy.'

Kirriemuir is a small Scottish town famous for being
birthplace to Peter Pan creator, J.M. Barrie, for ginger
bread and for being a hotbed of witchcraft in
the 16th century.

# P.J. Baker

## Northfield, Edinburgh

Once a proud Scot from Northfield,
One Hogmanay, ceilidhed and reeled,
When on Arthur's Seat a sea breeze
Lifted his kilt at the knees,
At midnight a true Scot was revealed!

In the east of Edinburgh, between the ancient volcano
Arthur's Seat and Portobello beach, lies Northfield. An
unremarkable place in a truly remarkable landscape.

# G.W. Colkitto

## Paisley

There was an old lecher from Paisley
Who took a new conquest to Disney
They went for a ride
She snuggled up to his side
She hoped he'd be good but he wisnae

Paisley is the largest town in Scotland, famous for
Paisley Pattern shawls, thread, and jam. Poetry is a
major part of its history with Robert Tannahill, the
weaver poet, pre-eminent.

# Joyce Colville Hart

## Elderslie

Stoddard's looms of old Elderslie
Made carpets for esteemed company:
From a wedding most regal,
To Epsom, Gleneagles,
And Regent Street's store, Liberty.


A chef born in wee Elderslie
Made a name for himself on TV
With his kitchen nightmares
Where he curses and swears
No, his taste really isn't for me.

Elderslie is a small village with a big history. Birthplace
to the Queen's wedding carpets, Braveheart and
Gordon Ramsay, it sits ten miles west of Glasgow.

# Sandy Inglis

## Gourdon, Montrose

A stunning young woman from Gourdon
led the life most deliciously wanton.
To ensnare married men
she'd lead them on then
make them pay through the nose with extortion.


A bothersome brat from Montrose
Was told to stop picking his nose
But he picked it then licked it
Rolled it then flicked it
For which he got several ASBOs

Gourdon is a working fishing village, one of the few
left in Scotland. Thomas Telford designed the harbour.
Montrose has the widest main street in Scotland and
the fifth oldest golf course in the world.

# Joan Lennon

## Newport-on-Tay, Fife

A lady who lived by the Tay
Found all older men *distingué* –
She pursued without pausing
Dapper OAPs, causing
Codgers to cry out, 'WAHAY!'


There was an old lady from Fife
Who said, looking back on her life,
'Though husbands are great
for the odd conjugate,
you're better off wedding a wife.'

The Kingdom of Fife is said to be shaped like the head
of a dog. If this is so, then the silvery Tay strokes it
most lovingly, every day.

# Fiona Strachan

## Johnshaven

A schoolboy in class in Johnshaven
Gave two fingers as if he was wavin'.
His signal in jest,
Earned him six of the best,
And detention for badly behavin'.

Johnshaven is a bonny coastal village located in
Aberdeenshire, and lies midway between Montrose
and Stonehaven. Once thriving on fishing, it is now a
holiday destination and artists' colony.

# The Limerati

## NORTH EAST

**Madeline Bennett** is a writer, blogger and mother-of-three living in Corbridge, Northumberland. She can be found at <www.writingbubble.co.uk>, where she ponders on parenthood and shares her poetry, prose and many limericks.

**Nick Brigham**, a resident of Hexham, has published two collections of his poems. Most of them reflect his unashamed preference for the old-fashioned virtues of rhyme and rhythm.

**Sylvia Bunting** of York has scribbled miscellaneous verses and stories all her life. Her writings include the book *Faces in the Crowd* and lyrics for the Bible musical, *Jairus' Daughter*.

**Anne Carmichael** of Morpeth, Northumberland writes for fun. Loves playing with words and rhymes. Influences: Nature and the changing seasons around her rural home. Success: One poem published in *Horse and Pony Annual 1979*!

**Alastair Chadwin** was born at Newcastle upon Tyne in 1964. Primarily a prose writer, he indulges in limericks and clerihews. This is his first published poem. Hopefully his last, he says.

**Steve Chettle** lives in Newburn. His birthday is 11th May; Edward Lear's is 12th May. This may explain a willingness to create a limerick/nonsense verse. He likes rivers and allotments.

**Kitty Fitzgerald** lives in Cullercoats and has had five novels published, most recently, *Identity* (July 2014, Room to Write) *Pigtopia* (Faber 2005) and short stories, *Miranda's Shadow* (IRON Press 2013).

**Christine D. Goodwin** of Whitley Bay: Northumberwoman, Modern Languages Teacher, Writer, Translator, Northumbrian Piper, Failed Poet, Photographer, Proud Mother, Dire Straits Fan, Great North Runner, Novice Ice-skater and Lover of Fairground Carousels.

**Oz Hardwick** lives in York, where he writes everything from poetry to music journalism to academic art history. His latest poetry collection is *The Ringmaster's Apprentice* (Valley Press, 2014)

**Doug Harris** of Stockton-on-Tees probably has the largest and finest collection of limerick books in Europe, possibly the world. Dating from as early as 1820, his collection is in several languages and continues to grow beyond 1500 items.

**Hugh Hunter** of Cleadon: Lucky enough to retire at 60 one year ago. Enrolled on first creative writing course through WEA in January. Discovering at every lesson that less is more.

**Andy Logan** of Tynemouth was born in Shropshire, but was Cullercoats-nurtured from the age of six and proud of it. He says he is a would-be jobbing poet.

**Margaret Nesbitt** of Berwick-upon-Tweed says she's had her three score years and ten, and life's been kind to her. There are memories, moments and precious times wrapped in words for the future to see.

**Orian Norfolk** of Dinnington, Newcastle, says he came to writing, and poetry, rather late in life and finds language rewarding; it is a joy to search for the right word, or explore the incongruous and absurd.

**Sean O'Brien** lives in Forest Hall and is a poet, critic, prose writer, editor, broadcaster, anthologist, and Professor of Creative Writing at Newcastle University. His most recent publication is *Collected Poems* (Picador 2012).

**June Portlock** of Wardley, Gateshead, says she's been lucky enough to have been published widely, including in an inhouse magazine for estate agents. Her collection, *Broken Biscuits,* was published by Diamond Twig.

**Joanna Rimmer** of Gosforth, Tyne & Wear spent twenty years living in the grounds of a mental hospital, before Canada, then finally Newcastle. She writes little but often – her first play was staged in July 2014 by Cloud Nine Theatre Company.

**Alison Ringrose** of Darras Hall, Ponteland is a language teacher who raised a family of three, puppy-walked twelve guide-dogs and feels it's now time to self-indulge! She belongs to Ponteland Writers Group and really enjoys writing.

**Fiona Ritchie Walker** of Blaydon is a Scot who's lived in NE England for over twenty years. Her poetry collections include *Garibaldi's Legs* (IRON Press) and *The Second Week of the Soap* (Red Squirrel Press). These are her first limericks since school.

**Chris Robinson** of Peterlee says she is an emerging poet and spoken word artist and her light-hearted approach to poetry, along with her performance style, allows her work to be enjoyed by all.

**Susan Routledge** of Hexham is sixty-one years old, and has been a member of a creative writing group for four years. She finds writing brings out a hidden side to her, a side she likes.

**Heather Ann Russell** of Dinnington Green started as a research biochemist, was later employed in-house as an editor, and subsequently became freelance. She now writes her own prize-winning poetry and prose, rather than editing that of others.

**Josephine Scott** of Cullercoats has an MA in Creative Writing from Northumbria University. Her first poetry collection, *Sparkle and Dance*, was published by Red Squirrel Press. Her second collection, *Rituals*, will be published in October 2014.

**Helen Shay** of Harrogate writes/performs poetry, teaches with York University CLL, presents events at festivals such as Ilkley Literature Festival, York Festival of Ideas and once guested at Glastonbury's Poets Tent – with mud stains to prove it.

**David Stephenson** of Greenside, Ryton is former assistant editor of IRON magazine and former publisher of The Bay Press. After a long hiatus earning a living, he is finally starting to write again.

**Rob Walton** of North Shields has had short fiction published in the IRON Press anthology, *Root*, and by Red Squirrel, New Writing North, Arachne and others. Poetry is a new thing. For him.

**Julian Wilkin** of Hexham has recently retired from working on rights-of-way in Northumberland. He says his creative writing class tutor, Clair, keeps presenting them with poetry, which stretches him somewhat.

**Evelyn Ann Williams** of Fulwell, has enjoyed writing poetry for many years but this has previously been reserved for family and friends. This is her first attempt at publication.

# MIDLANDS

**Julie Burke** of West Bridgford, Nottingham loves writing poetry – has had some published – but although she especially enjoys writing silly, funny rhymes, she's always found limericks tricky. So, she's particularly thrilled to be included here.

**Tracy Davidson** lives near Stratford-on-Avon. Her poems have appeared in various publications including: *Mslexia, Atlas Poetica, Roundyhouse, Modern Haiku* and *The Right-Eyed Deer*.

**Helen Everett-Camplin** of Oakham, says she is more 'Witty Dittier' than Poet. She adores leading orchestras of words in rousing choruses of rollicking rhythms and rampant rhymes, the more raucous the better, hence her love of limericks.

**Cindy George** is a writer who accidentally fell into poetry – and Coventry – while doing an MA at Warwick University. She's a big fan of 'people's poetry' like limericks and ballads.

**Allison Heward** of Morda is an actress/published writer. She'd love to say these occupations get her a living wage, but to pay the bills she also works full time in special education.

**Rennie Parker** lives in Stamford, Lincs. Her latest collection *Candleshoe* was published by Shoestring Press earlier this year. It doesn't include any poems about footwear.

**D. A. Prince** of Kirby Muxloe, Leicester, relishes both light verse and the weightier variety. Her second collection from HappenStance Press, *Common Ground*, was published in 2014.

**Dennis Walker** of Oakham is a retired law lecturer with an interest in all forms of writing. In addition to poetry successes he has had comedy sketches produced on radio and television.

## East Anglia

**Catherine Bailey** of Drayton has always loved writing in all its forms and tends to draw on her wealth of memories to generate quintessential British humour in all her stories and verse.

**Lois Williams** of Dersingham has loved limericks since childhood. Usually she writes about history and nature. Her work has appeared in *Verse Daily, New England Review, Antiphon, The Rotary Dial*, and *Granta*.

## London

**Annemarie Cooper** of London, E1 is a poet and gardener whose collection *The Flight of Birds* came out in spring 2013.

**Gerda Mayer** lives in Chingford, E4. Her latest collection of poems appeared in translation in Norway, in 2013. Also still in print are her *Bernini's Cat* (IRON Press) and *Prague Winter*. She writes for children and adults.

## South East

**Paula Balfe** of Southend-on-Sea is a nurse, complementary therapist and entrepreneurial knitter. Her writing has appeared in literary magazines including *Iota, Brand* and *Obsessed with Pipework* plus three anthologies. She is currently working on her first collection.

**Michael Charles** of Gravesend, Kent was Head of English in a comprehensive school. Poetry allowed him to tap into the children's creativity. Now that he is retired he writes his own poems.

**Frances Chatt** of Thornton Heath, Surrey recently retired and decided to try writing again – a hobby when she was much younger. She enjoys experimenting with poetic forms and the limericks got her started.

**Simon John Cox** of Tunbridge Wells has a job in marketing, a degree in chemistry and a black belt in Taekwon-Do, and has been writing for longer than he cares to remember.

**Nicollette Foreman** of Chelmsford has been writing since 2008, and has been published in *Sentinel Poetry Movement*; *Dawntreader*; *Pre-Raphaelite Society* and further anthologies and loves to write in different styles and genres.

**Dee Gordon** of Southend-on-Sea: Her writing has focussed on local history. However, *Bad Girls*, a poetry collection, did well for accolades, and other poems have won a number of competitions and prizes. Website <www.deegordon-writer.com>.

**Anne Murphy** of Chelmsford started writing poems about ten years ago, and the things still won't leave her alone. They mostly come at night... mostly...

**Marion Russell** of Rochester, Kent says that at seventy-six her only claim to poetry fame has been writing poems for her two children's A level practice (for which she got 'A' grades). Now the limerick is for her!

**Patricia Feinberg Stoner** of Rustington is a former journalist and publicist now retired and an active member of a local creative writing group. Author of *Paws and Whiskers* (available on Kindle), a collection of humorous cat verses.

**John Whitworth** of Canterbury has published ten poetry books which, he says, is far too many. *Girlie Gangs* is his latest from Enitharmon. Les Murray likes it. Good on him!

**Kevin Wooldridge** of Rayners Lane, Pinner thinks the short story is king, though he enjoys writing comic poetry. A novel is 'in development' – when published it will be dedicated to the late Paul Torday.

## SOUTH

**Sue Spiers** of Southampton is treasurer of OU Poets and has poems on The Writing Hampshire Poetry Map. She says she adores irreverent rhythm and rhyme, so often absent in contemporary poetry.

**Allison Symes** of Eastleigh, Hants writes fairytales with bite, usually as novels and short stories, but adores flirting with poems and radio scripts. Allison's favourite authors are P.G.Wodehouse, Jane Austen and Terry Pratchett.

**Janet Turner** of New Forest, Hants says she is inspired while buzzing around the New Forest on her electric buggy, to write children's stories and poetry (from silly to serious), some of which have been published/won prizes – busy old bee!

## SOUTH WEST

**Jerome Betts** lives in breezy cliff-perched St. Marychurch, which still wonders if annexation in 1900 by balmy palmy Torquay, which allegedly coveted its steamroller, was quite such a good move.

**Maggie Bevan** is retired by the sea in Devon, where she writes stories, paints in acrylic, and surveys the county from top decks of buses while earwigging strangers' conversations.

**Phyllis Higgins** of Frome likes to enter competitions and has been short-listed several times. Some of her poems have appeared in anthologies. She also performs her poetry in Frome.

**Moira Quinn** of Penzance says that words to change the world are what started and keep her writing, along with rhythm, lyricism, the ethereal, the magical and a big slice of nonsense; there's always room for that.

**Caroline Rose** of Frome has delighted in words since she was a child, doing everything from crosswords through stories to poems. She says that unfortunately, she's never learnt to spell, so VIVA spell-check!

**Jill Sharp** of Swindon tutors for the Open University and runs creative writing groups. She enjoys hill-walking, singing, dancing and playing hide-and-seek. Her poems have appeared in magazines and anthologies.

**Janet Lesley Smith** was born in Cambridge, in 1940. After a life involving periods abroad, she has lived in Frome for twenty-eight years, where she enjoys writing poetry as a hobby.

**Natalie Smith** of Bristol is a published short story writer and produced playwright. Her brevity in writing is aided by vats of tea and vast quantities of chilli chocolate.

**Helen Somers**, a member of Writers in Somerset and a local of Burnham-on-Sea as both her grandparents are buried there, lives with husband, dog and various chickens, near the coast.

**Dr Bob Turvey** of Stoke Bishop: happily married 40 years; keen student of the history of limericks; owner of a cat that looks like Hitler; retired research chemist; published children's book writer.

**Jane Wheble** of Hereford likes putting things together: fabric scraps for quilts, word scraps for poems. Jiggling them around until they fit.

## WALES

**Mary Halliwell** of Rhos on Sea worked at Bangor Museum until recent retirement. She says she's always written silly verse, as her long-suffering friends would confirm, but she does write some serious stuff too.

**Shirley Hammond-Williams** of Bosherston is a cat and country lover. She enjoys writing poems of various genres to entertain, reflect a mood or encapsulate a moment in time. Also likes turning stories into ballads.

## NORTH WEST

**Jane Allsop** (of Burton in Kendal) is a writer of verse, whose rhyming is sometimes perverse. She lives near the Lakes, eats too many cakes and has dwelt in countries diverse.

**Sue Barnard**, once described by her son as 'professionally weird', has lived in Hale for over thirty years. She is a poet, editor, and novelist.

**David Bateman** of Liverpool has more limericks in *Curse Of The Killer Hedge* (IRON Press 1996). He also edited the Liverpool poetry anthology, *The Dead Good Poets Society: The Book* (Headland 2005).

**John Calvert** is a writer, performer, musician and freelance educationalist living in Levenshulme, Manchester. He likes prog rock, old railway lines and coffee.

**David Crossley** of Lytham St Annes is retired and has lived in Lytham for nine years. His inspiration for writing anything at all comes from his wife Rita, an avid writer herself.

**Christine Henderson** has lived in Lancashire for thirty years, five of them in Carnforth. Now retired, and with more time for writing, she's enjoying seeing some of her efforts appearing in print.

**Gordon Hill** of Huyton came late to writing, having spent a lifetime in the motor trade, trying to get something to rhyme with Lamborghini. A case of bonnets to sonnets perhaps.

**Jim Lewis** of Boughton, Chester is a freelance writer. He enjoys spending his spare time in one of Chester's 17th century inns, sporting renaissance-style facial hair and composing funny rhymes.

## Scotland

**Stephanie Arsoska** of Kirriemuir is published in *An Anthology of Motherhood* (The Emma Press) and was commended in the Mother's Milk writing competition. She writes for *Word Bohemia* and *BritMums* and blogs at <www.beautifulmisbehaviour.com>.

**P.J. Baker** of Edinburgh enjoys writing funny rhyming poems for children and adults. This is her second poem chosen for an anthology.

**G.W. Colkitto** of Paisley writes poetry and prose. In poetry he likes all forms: free verse, traditional rhyme and metre, concrete. More of his poetry can be found at <www.gwcolkitto.co.uk>.

**Joyce Colville Hart** of Elderslie has only recently begun to write and perform poetry. This is her first published verse. She is a retired maths teacher so is accomplished at counting – poetic metre included!

**Sandy Inglis** of Gourdon is a member of Inverbervie Writers Group and enjoys writing poetry, much of which is written in Doric, the native tongue of North East Scotland.

**Joan Lennon** of Newport-on-Tay. As primarily a fiction writer, Joan is embarrassed to admit that one of the things she loves about poetry is the word count. Not easier – just shorter!

**Fiona Strachan** of Johnshaven says she is a former drama teacher, now failed children's author, who has achieved a modicum of success writing bits and pieces of poetic nonsense in local Doric dialect. She's plodding on.